LEKEYANTIA NAYLOR

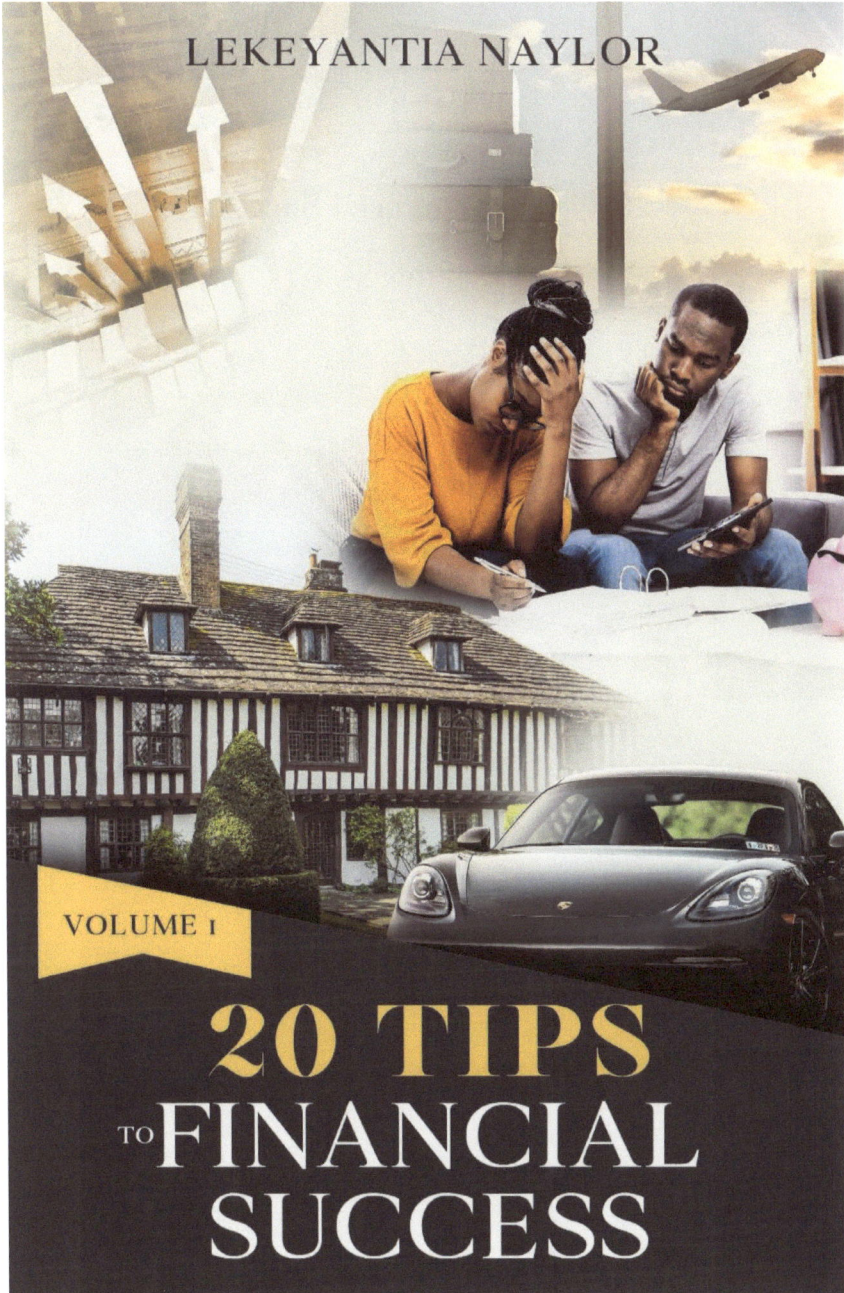

VOLUME I

20 TIPS
TO FINANCIAL
SUCCESS

20 Tips To Financial Success
Volume 1

BY

Lekeyantia Naylor

THELNBOOKS
MEMPHIS, TN

20 TIPS TO FINANCIAL SUCCESS VOL. 1

Copyright © 2021 Lekeyantia Naylor

Forward

This book was written mostly because the Holy Spirit instructed me to do so. I told myself, once my youngest child started kindergarten that I would look for another job to give me something to do and bring more income into the household. Once school started, I began my job search, but the hours just did not work for our situation. Also, I just did not want to clock in for anyone and work all those hours to make someone else's dreams come true instead of mine. So, one day I asked God, of my many talents, to give me something I can do and will enjoy doing that can also be a source of income for my family. Then, maybe a week later, I was in bed and suddenly he told me to write this book. He gave me the title, some of the tips, and even told me how to go about doing it; so, I began right away.

Over the years, I have been asked by numerous people to give them advice, tips, and to show them how we have been able to accomplish everything we have accomplished financially as well as in other areas.

This book is a beginner's blueprint of how we got started and the things we did along the way to get to where we are today. Hopefully, it can be for others what it has been for us and that is a tool to help you have a successful financial future.

ABOUT THE AUTHOR

Lekeyantia Naylor is the mother of two beautiful children, a son Eric Jr. (7), and a daughter Constance (5). Lekeyantia was born in Chicago, Illinois on August 27, 1993, and raised in Flint, Michigan until the age of fourteen. She and her family moved to Oxford, Mississippi until she graduated high school in 2011. She graduated Magna Cum Laude in 2019 with an Associate's Degree in Applied Science in Paralegal Studies from Southwest Tennessee Community College. She enjoys dancing, traveling the world, visiting new places, and experiencing new adventures with her family.

Lekeyantia has a heart for people and cares about those who are less fortunate, which led to her starting her own non-profit in 2019, Yahweh Yireh Organization (yahwehyirehmemphis.org) to fight homelessness in Memphis, Tennessee.

Acknowledgements

Thank you, God, for all the gifts and talents you have blessed me with. Thank you for keeping me in your hedge of protection, the favor over my life, and giving me the vision to complete my first book.

I want to thank Eric for supporting, helping, encouraging, and praying with me.

Thank you to my beautiful children for motivating me every day. Thank you for giving me a reason to be a better all-around person and mother. I hope I have been a great example for you as you continue growing.

Thank you to my best friend, Kayla Payton, for all the love, support, encouragement, ideas, prayers, being my personal hype woman, and sometimes believing in me more than I did in myself.

I also want to give a huge thank you to the following people who have helped us in some way over the years when we were in need financially or needed financial guidance. Whether it was in the form of small financial blessings, furniture, or information and resources to point us in the right direction, it all is greatly appreciated. Brandon and Colanda Underwood, Cassandra Dillon, Torrence and Kahillia Myers, Rolland and Wendy Turner, Barrett and India Watson.

Thank you, DesTine Bell, for being an amazing photographer and listening to all my ideas, and being able to make my vision come to life.

Finally, thank you, Seletha Head-Tucker, for your hard work and for doing an amazing job making this book become a reality.

**If I have forgotten anyone, please charge it to my head, not my heart.

TABLE OF CONTENTS

Tip #1

Put God in your Finances

This may sound like a cliché, but WHEN you put God in the middle of your finances, it helps tremendously. You do this by developing a REAL relationship with God through prayer, studying His Word, and creating relationships with other like-minded believers. This is the most helpful tip. WHY? Because on the road to financial success, there are going to be lots of ups and downs. And, you must have faith that God is going to work things out in your favor and give you wisdom in what you should do next. If you try to do this without God, you may end up operating from a place of desperation and end up in a worse financial state than you were before. This is where a lot of people make the most financial mistakes.

Tip #2

Tithe

Most people don't believe in Tithing or perhaps have some crazy stories to tell about it. But, I have seen firsthand how important tithing is for your finances. When my husband and I first moved out on our own, we were not involved in church and did not have any financial tools to guide us. After about a year and a half of living on our own, we started going to church faithfully but we were not tithing. We would give $5 here, $10 there, and if we really wanted to feel like we were doing something, maybe $20 another week. But most of the time, we gave nothing at all because we felt like we could not afford to tithe. We felt we needed to make sure we had enough for groceries, gas, and other necessities. So, we just gave God what we had left if anything. When we lived like this, we found ourselves never having enough or just getting by. One day my husband said, "we need to start tithing our 10% no matter what". I agreed. So, every time we got paid, before we paid any bills, we would tithe our 10% to church FIRST and then pay our bills afterward.

It was hard in the beginning but as time passed, we noticed our finances started to become less of a burden.

Suddenly my husband was getting raises, promotions, checks from places saying they owe us money, and big bonuses. Things we did not even know were available to us started happening once we started trusting God with our finances FOR REAL!

Tip #3

Do Not Make Financial Decisions When Coming from a Place of Desperation

The worst time to make any decisions, especially financial decisions, is when you are feeling desperate or rushed. NEVER, I repeat NEVER make big and/or important decisions when you have not had adequate time to pray about it and think on it. No matter how good the offer sounds, if the person or establishment will not allow you time to weigh out your options on a financial matter, then most likely it was not for you to begin with.

> For example: There was a time years ago before we had a real relationship with God that we were in desperate need of a new car. We were still financially immature at that time. So, we decided to go to a dealership to look at some used cars. Somehow, they talked us into getting a brand-new car. The price was not too bad, around $18,000, but when it came time for our final signatures for the car after financing and interest, the purchase price of the car was $31,000. The interest rate was 14.44% with a car note of $445.74!

I did not want us to sign on the dotted line and commit to that payment, but we both felt we had no other option (desperate and rushed); so, we signed. We had no idea how we were going to pay that every month on our budget.

But despite our mistake and poor judgment, God made a way every month for us to be able to pay our bills on time and sometimes ahead of time. We never had a delinquent payment.

Tip #4

Develop Financial Wisdom

It is especially important to be able to make financially smart decisions for yourself and/or your family. You must really evaluate yourself. If you know you are someone who lacks wisdom in certain areas, then ask God to give you wisdom. If you are unable to do this on your own, it may be helpful to ask someone you trust and know who has financial wisdom to help you come up with a plan to get you started on the right path. It is also helpful to know the end goal or vision you want for a project, your life, or your business. Without a vision of what you want, it will be extremely hard to make a solid financial plan to reach your goals. You must be able to discern what will be beneficial and/or harmful to what it is you are trying to accomplish. If you are married or have a partner, then you will want to sit down and figure out who is best at making financial decisions and have them take charge in that area. Play to each other's strengths. It is NOT a competition; you are a team.

Tip #5

Write Down Your Plans/Vision

The Bible tells us in Habakkuk 2:2-3: *Then the Lord said to me, "Write the vision plainly on tablets, so that a runner can carry the correct message to others. This vision is for a future time. It describes the end, and it will be fulfilled. If it seems slow in coming, wait patiently, for it will surely take place. It will not be delayed."*

This is a particularly important and helpful tip. When you and/or your spouse finally come up with a plan or vision, get a computer or notebook and write it down in complete detail. It should consist of what you want it to be, how you want it to look, how you plan to make it happen, and a potential date of completion. Sometimes, what you write down will not happen exactly as you had planned, but it will be a guide and give you a way to track your progress.

> For example: My husband and I decided we wanted to buy a house, but we were not in a position to do so at the time. So, we sat down and made a list of everything that needed to be done to buy our first home. The list had things such as paying off debt, getting a credit score of 640, saving X amount of money, and taking a down payment assistance class. We gave ourselves a realistic goal to have it done by the time our son turned five. At that time, he was about one ½ years old.

We knocked out everything one by one and we were able to purchase our first home when our son was three years old.

Writing things down makes a world of difference. So, WRITE THE VISION, MAKE IT PLAIN!

Tip #6

Write Down Income and Expenses

On your financial journey, you will learn how important it is to write things down! One of the first things you will want to do is to create a biweekly and/or monthly income/expense spreadsheet. You can do this in your notebook or computer. This will give you a rough estimate of how much you make and an idea of how much you spend or should have left over after bills. When making your monthly income section of the spreadsheet, only put your minimum net income. So, if you work full time, put how much a flat 80-hour check would be with no overtime or bonuses included.

By going off your minimum income, it shows you exactly where you are financially and if you can pay all your essential recurrent bills with or without overtime. If you happen to be in the negative, it is not the end of the world. You can still achieve financial success; it will just take a little more work and sacrifice. If you are fortunate enough NOT to be in the negative using your minimum income, then when you do work extra hours, it gives you more opportunities to get to where you want to be. When you start to write down all your expenses, only write down the essential recurrent bills needed to survive nothing extra, and always estimate high.

For example: Light, gas, and water bills fluctuate, so think back to your highest most recent bill and put that number down as your monthly amount. That way, if one month is significantly lower, you have the extra money in your budget to pay down debt or pay off another bill.

Another example: If you have kids and it is time to go school shopping, or you need a new tire one week, just add it to your expense list for that pay period. You will then add it all together and subtract it from your net income to get the total amount you will have remaining that week to go towards debt. If you worked overtime or you are expecting extra money from somewhere, then that will just be extra left to pay off a bigger amount of debt. If you are in the negatives, then your overtime money will take care of the negative balance, and anything left over will pay off or pay on a debt.

On the next few pages are two examples of how to create your income/expense spreadsheet. Both examples are two-income families but with completely different expenses. No matter how small the amount you have remaining or how much you make, you can still use it to save, pay off debt, or student loans. After creating this, most people will be shocked to see how much money they have left over but never see it. This happens because they spend their money on unnecessary things. But, if you can go a year just following this budget, you will see how much you can achieve when you are willing to sacrifice unimportant things to achieve your goal.

Example 1 (Family of 4 with no government assistance)	
Monthly Income	**Monthly Expenses**
$3,100	Tithe $310
	Rent/Mortgage $700
	Phone $100
	Cable $70
	Car/Life Insurance $200
	Car Note $350
	Lights/Gas/Water Bill $200
	Groceries $600
	Car Gas $100
	Money Left in account till next check $200
Total	**$2,830**

Example 1 (Family of 4 with no government assistance)	
Biweekly Income	**Biweekly Expenses**
Check #1 (End of the Month) $1,550	Tithe $155
	Rent/Mortgage $700
	Car/Life Insurance $200
	Groceries $300
	Car Gas $50
	Money left in account for unexpected needs $100
Total	**$1,505 ($45 Remaining)**
Check #2 (Beginning of the Month) $1,550	Tithe $155
	Car Note $350
	Light/Gas/Water Bill $200
	Groceries $300
	Car Gas $50

	Phone Bill $100
	Cable $70
	Money left in account for unexpected needs $100
Total	**$1,325 ($225 Remaining)**

Example 2 (Family of 4 with government assistance)	
Monthly Income	**Monthly Expenses**
$1,680	Tithe $168
	Rent/Mortgage $400
	Phone $86
	Cable $45
	Lights/Gas/Water $102
	Groceries (Food Stamps)
	Car Gas $250
	Money Left in account till next check $200
Total	**$1,251**

Example 2 (Family of 4 with government assistance)	
Biweekly Income	**Biweekly Expenses**
Check #1 (End of the Month) $840	Tithe $84
	Rent/Mortgage $400
	Groceries (Food Stamps)
	Car Gas $125
	Money left in account for unexpected needs $100
Total	**$709 ($131 Remaining)**
Check #2 (Beginning of the Month) $840	Tithe $84
	Light Bill $102
	Groceries (Food Stamps)
	Car Gas $125
	Phone Bill $86
	Cable $45
	Money left in account for unexpected needs $100
Total	**$542 ($298 Remaining)**

Tip #7

Have Discipline

The road to financial success is HARD and it requires a tremendous amount of self-discipline. Depending on the timeframe you would like to accomplish your goals will determine how much sacrifice and discipline is required to get it. Discipline means if you have set a goal to let's say buy your first home in the next year or two, and you want to save $10,000 for a down payment or closing cost. Depending on your financial situation, you will have to make a commitment to yourself to either limit, or completely go without whatever you have in your budget that is robbing you of extra money, such as fast food, alcohol, cigarettes, shopping, parties, or frequent trips. You will have to learn how to say no to people and temporarily deny yourself of small simple luxuries to experience your life on another level and complete your goals. This is one of the MOST important and difficult steps. It is virtually impossible to accomplish any financial goals without having discipline. The vision you have for your future must be worth the wait and far more important to you than the things you desire to do and have right now.

Tip #8

Utilize Your Calendar

Everyone who has a cell phone has access to a calendar, but many hardly use it, especially the ones who really need to. In my case, I usually have many things I need to get done, or my mind is always on 1,000. So, it is necessary to put things on my calendar to remind me about important things, such as when all bills are due, or maybe when the air filter needs changing. Other people are just extremely forgetful or irresponsible and need to be reminded of everything. Whatever the reason, utilizing your calendar can really help you get on track to being more responsible and it is very convenient and helpful. If you don't already, start using your calendar. The first thing you want to do is ensure all your essential recurrent bills' due dates are on your calendar that you listed on your expense sheet. Then, the night before you get paid, have your calendar up to ensure you have all essential and nonrecurrent bills accounted for in that pay period. Then, calculate everything to find out how much will be left over to go towards debt. What I mean by nonrecurrent bills is, anything like car tags, or you have a doctor's appointment that requires a copay, or you need an oil change. Make sure to put anything that requires you to spend money into your calendar, so you don't forget. I know this may sound crazy or excessive, but it helps tremendously.

Tip #9

Improve Your Credit Score

Credit is something most people have heard about, but don't really know much about it, or no one has really educated them on the subject enough for them to make good decisions pertaining to it. I know this was the case for us, but once you know what to do, what to expect, and how to navigate your credit, it becomes quite easy to manage. When I first started my credit journey back in 2013 my credit was 476, but that was because I had little to no credit, and the credit I did have were student loans from a semester of college I took in 2011, and a couple of doctor bills. Now my credit score sits at 803.

The first step to repairing your credit is knowing what your credit score is, and what is currently on your credit report that is negatively impacting it. You can find this by creating a Credit Karma account or any other platform that allows you to check your credit for free. Once you have created an account with someone and have access to your credit report, the next thing you are going to want to do first is to write down everything that is under derogatory marks (if using Credit Karma) and anything else you have an outstanding balance on under total accounts.

Derogatory marks have a high impact on your score and should be paid off first when you start paying off debt, usually starting with the small balances first and saving the bigger debts for last. You start with the small balances first because they can be paid off faster and will have a greater impact on your credit when you have multiple accounts being paid off back-to-back. If you have credit cards that you owe a balance on, pay those down next. Never have multiple credit cards in use especially for substantial amounts when you know you will not be able to pay them off fully in the next 30 days. When paying off your credit cards, if you do not have a credit card with a 0% introductory APR or it has recently expired, then you will want to pay off the credit card with the highest interest rate as fast as possible and then go from there. The credit card(s) with the 0% APR can be paid off last because they are not building interest. Also, keep in mind that you still must make your minimum payment on them every month (usually $35). Make sure to write down when the introductory period ends so you can try to have the balance paid before the interest kicks in.

Next, check out your hard inquiries. These have a minimal impact on your credit and fall off every 2 years, but if you have too many, it can hurt your credit. So, try to keep inquiries on your credit to a minimum (between 2 and 4) and only apply for things that you really need. Another thing to remember is that your credit score will fluctuate. Sometimes it will make small dips and sometimes big ones depending on what you have paid off or added to your credit; DO NOT FREAK OUT. If you are doing the things you are supposed to be doing, it's okay and will come back up soon. Sometimes it takes a long time for credit bureaus to update your information so just be patient and it will show up. If you have paid off something and it seems to be taking too long, just call the company or entity and ask them to report your updated information to the credit bureaus. You can also ask for a paid-in-full letter to be sent to you just in case you need to dispute anything in the future.

Tip #10

Pay Off Debt

Once you know where your credit stands, have everything written down, know your budget, and are ready to start working towards your financial goals, the next step is to start paying off your debt. You can do this by referring to your income and expenses spreadsheet. For every check you receive, write down your expenses for that pay period and subtract it from your net income. With the money you have left, no matter how big or small, pay it towards one of your debts from the list you created when you looked at your credit report. This is when having discipline will come into play. Let's say you worked hard and did some overtime and to God be the glory you paid all your bills due this pay period. You bought groceries and have gas money, and $100 for anything that may come up between now and your next check. When you calculate, you see you have $700 left over to pay off some debt, or to pay off one or a couple in full. You will have to have the discipline, willpower, and financial wisdom to take that money and put it towards something that is going to help your future self and not take that money to go out or buy things that you want right now. The more you do this, the easier it will become, and when you start to see your debt continue to decrease, it will encourage you to keep going until you finally get to that last payment before you are finally debt-free.

Tip #11

Use Income Tax Money Wisely

One of the biggest mistakes many people make is when it comes to their income tax. Most of the time people take that money and spend it on clothes, shoes, TVs, cars, vacations, etc. and that is ok. But, when you are not where you want to be financially, or not where you want to be in life, it is not the best way to use your money. If you are single, it makes it a little easier in a way because you only have to worry about yourself. When my husband and I started our financial journey, we agreed that every year we would take our income tax and pay off our debt. Since there were two of us with debt, we started with the breadwinner, my husband, because our goal was to buy a house in the next couple of years and his income would be what helped us get it, so we wanted his credit to match his finances. Also, he had significantly more debt than me, so it just made more sense.

The first year his student loans garnished our taxes because we kept putting off paying them not knowing that if we had just made one payment it would have stopped that from happening. We were devastated, but it worked out in our favor because that student loan was in collections (derogatory marks) and hurting his credit so that being almost completely paid off, shot his credit up. After that happened, we set up payment plans for both of us to ensure that would not happen again and it would also be helping us pay down a debt. So, the next year we used it to pay off the rest of his debt and a little of mine while throughout the year using our checks to pay off smaller debts. It only took us two years to pay off all our debt leaving just our student loans to continue paying monthly. Using our income taxes this way helped us take care of things at a much faster pace and having lump sums allowed us to pay off more debt at a time.

Tip #12

Apply For Only One Credit Card

Once you have paid down your debt and have a responsible financial groove going, you are going to want to apply for a credit card. At this point, your credit should be good enough to apply for a regular credit card like in our case, a Capital One Platinum credit card. If not, then try applying for a secure credit card or holding off on this step for a little bit longer until you pay off a couple more things on your credit report. Credit Karma usually gives you a good idea of where you are approval-wise with a variety of different credit cards so pay attention to that. If your approval odds are exceptionally good ("very good" is the term credit karma uses), then it is a good chance you will get the credit card. Always look at the perks like rewards, travel, or cash back cards and see if they have welcome bonuses. If possible, try and go for a card with a 0% intro APR (usually between 14 and 18 months) and a $0 annual fee.

Do not go applying for credit cards back-to-back because remember you do not want a lot of inquiries on your credit report and besides, you only need one at a time. Before committing to a credit card make sure you compare it to others and base it on what you plan to use it for, and how often you plan to use it, then make your decision from that.

For example, when we got our first card the credit limit was only $500 and we used it for small expenses, things we were going to buy anyway like groceries for the next two weeks, and instead of using cash we left it on the account and used the credit card instead. After a couple of days when the grocery charge was posted, we would then take that cash in our account and use it to pay our credit card off in full. We also did this for gas, school shopping, and sometimes bills. Using it for things that were already on our expense sheet ensured we would have the money to pay it off because we had already put it in our budget and all while building up our credit.

Make sure when you get your first card you find out how often you can request a credit limit increase (usually every 6 months) and if you are using it regularly and paying it off on time make sure you request one every time. Higher credit limits also improve your credit score. If you choose to get another credit card later, make sure you take the same steps you did in picking the first one with your next one as well. In the future when you really get the hang of it, know what you are doing, and have freed up some of your finances then you can start using them for bigger purchases, but we won't get into that right now.

Tip #13

Always Check Interest Rates

Interest rates SUCK. They can turn a good deal into a horrible one in a split second. It is important you know what your interest rates are and how much they are adding to whatever it is you are getting or purchasing. As I mentioned earlier, when we went to the dealership to purchase a car the price started out at $18,000 and ended up being $31,000 after $10,200 in interest and other charges were added. After that horrible deal, we made sure we did not make that mistake again so, when we went to get our next car, our credit was much better and so was our interest rate. Our next car was newer and because we did not get it completely brand new this time and our credit was better, we got it preowned with only 13,000 miles; it saved us thousands! Our interest rate went all the way down to 4.19% adding only $2,000 to the total of the car, which was $22,700; an enormous difference! It is the same thing with your credit cards or if you are purchasing a house, ALWAYS CHECK YOUR INTEREST RATES!

Tip #14

Have An Emergency Fund

Having an emergency fund is extremely important, but most people do not have one and when something happens, they panic and make decisions that will hurt them in the future. Therefore, it is wise to figure out how much you and/or your family would need in the event of an emergency.

> For example, when I created a breakdown of one of our savings, it consisted of 4 things: $1,000 for our comprehensive deductibles, $1,000 for our collision deductibles for both of our cars in the event of an accident, $1,658 for our home deductible in the event anything happened to our home, and finally $1,000 for any unexpected emergency that requires money such as needing a new water heater or copay if someone needed to go to the emergency room. In total, that's $4,658 that should not be touched unless there was an emergency.

Having an emergency fund gives you peace of mind when unexpected situations happen and the ability to keep a clear mind to make sound decisions. This is another situation where discipline and financial wisdom mentioned earlier are so important. You must use them every day, and it takes a HUGE amount of discipline to have that kind of money in savings and never touch or look at it unless necessary. In the event of an emergency, it also requires you to use wisdom to know how and when to spend your money. Now you may not be able to do this right away if you are still working on things previously mentioned and that is ok, but at least try to have something put away in case of an emergency.

Tip #15

Have at Least Two Savings Accounts

If you have a tough time keeping up with your money or you just like things to be organized and in their place, I suggest creating at least 2 savings accounts as well as having your checking account.

> For example, you can have one savings strictly for your mortgage/rent money, and in our case, we have it set for autopay so as long as we know how many months' worth is in there, that's one less bill we need to worry about. We simply write down when it is due or put a reminder in our calendar. The other savings can be for your emergency fund mentioned earlier.

Another thing that can be helpful is if you have a small portion of your check (like 5%) go into each account, that way with every check you are slowly building your emergency fund as well as your mortgage/rent money for the next month! This just leaves your checking account with the smaller bills and spending money. If you feel you want to have all your bill money in one savings just make sure you know the monthly total for all your bills and make sure that your account always has that amount or more to cover them. That way your checking account will just be pure spending money or if you still have debt, it will be your left-over money to take care of that. Doing this makes it a little easier instead of all your money occupying one account.

Tip #16

Make Yearly Goals/Vision Boards

Make yearly goals and vision boards and place them somewhere in your house where it can be seen daily. It can be greatly beneficial to wake up every morning and walk past it to remind yourself of what you are working so hard for. It also keeps you motivated and prevents distractions. You can do one or the other or both.

We started doing goals/vision boards in 2017 and it was nothing complex just a poster board with 3 columns. The first column listed all the goals we wanted to achieve that year and they varied from spiritual goals, debt goals, health goals, personal goals, financial goals, school goals, etc.

The second column was our blessing column. So, as best as we could, we wrote down every blessing no matter how small that happened to us throughout the year, and they varied from raises at work, being given a ton of furniture for our apartment, money saved with childcare, when someone helped us get food for the week, when we bought our first home, and when God gave me wisdom regarding our finances; just to name a few.

The third column consisted of dates we wanted to go on together because we had been lacking in that area and wanted to do better. Every year after that we would sit down and talk about what we wanted to do in the next year and write it down on another poster board. Some goals and dates we were unable to complete or get to from the previous year, so we just carried them over to the next year until it was accomplished.

You can also use photos of things you want, in 2019 I made a personal vision board just for me, and I used pictures of the different goals I had for myself.

I had pictures of different businesses I wanted to start, my dream car, different ways I wanted to grow emotionally and as a person, and a lot of the things came to pass. Then one day, years later, I went into my closet and pulled out all our old vision boards and began to read all our goals, and blessings to see how far we had come, and everything we had accomplished and overcame, and it was an amazing feeling.

I was even able to go back and cross some things off that had been accomplished. Doing this yearly can really be inspirational not only to you but others you may share it with. Yearly goals and vision boards help you see where you were, where you are, and where you want to be.

Tip #17

Make a Financial To-Do List

It is one thing to just say you have a financial plan and to-do list, but it is another thing entirely when you have taken the time to think and write it all down. There are many ways you can create a financial plan/to-do list, it is up to you how you want to go about it. For example, the easiest way may be to start out month by month. You would start with whatever month you are in and write down financial goals or goals, in general, you would like to complete by the end of that month, and each month after, until you make it to your end goal. The longer you do this and the better you get at it; you may want to switch to yearly goals. Breaking your yearly financial goals into smaller sections throughout the year makes it easier for you to focus on a smaller number of things at a time and can make it less overwhelming. Once your finances free up more and you have figured out your financial rhythm, yearly goals may become more ideal for you. The next page is an example.

Monthly Financial To-Do List	
January	• Pay $200 towards hospital bill • Put $150 in savings
February	• Pay $200 towards student loans • Put $200 in savings
March	• Use tax money to pay up on mortgage/rent and car note • Put $400 towards paying up the light bill

Tip #18

Pay Your Bills Up for The Year

When you have taken care of all your debt and no longer owe anyone, try to start paying your bills ahead. You don't have to jump right into paying them up for the year if you can just start paying some a couple of months in advance and see the relief it gives you. Make a table (refer to the table on the next page) of all your essential bills and calculate how much they cost for the entire year. You may be surprised at how low some are. For some bills, you can pay over the amount due, and it will create a credit on your account, that way when the next bill is due you will not have to worry about it, it will just pay the amount due from the credit in your account. Once you calculate how much the bill is for the year you can keep adding little by little to the account credit, or when you get the full amount, apply it all to the account and you will not have to worry about that bill for the entire year. Just remember to write it down and put it in your calendar when that bill will be due. Other bills will not allow you to pay ahead or create an account credit so, in those cases, you will just put that money into your savings account and pull from that account monthly to pay those bills or set up auto pay and allow it to come out of the savings automatically.

When you get to the point where you can pay your bills yearly, that opens your finances up tremendously! Now, every time you get your paycheck instead of it going towards bills you have the freedom to do the things you desire such as traveling, starting a business, etc. Remember, to keep this going, you must continue to add money to your savings or account credits, so you don't end up paying bills monthly all over again, it is important to continue to practice financial discipline and financial wisdom. To do this, you may want to increase the percentage going into your savings accounts to 10% in each account and 10% to tithe, and that still leaves you with 70% of your check to make big moves with. Now, if your bills require more than that then just adjust the percentage to match what you need. If you want to ensure you will no longer have to worry at all about bills, then figure out what percentage of your check you can live off and put the rest into your accounts. That way, bills are always covered and if a business or traveling opportunities present itself, you will know you have the money to cover it.

2025 Financial To-Do List		
Mortgage Savings	$8,400.00 per year minimum (@ $700.00 per month)	Complete Next Bill Due Jan 2026
Car Note	$4,200.00 per year (@$350.00 per month)	Not Complete Next Bill Due July 2025
Phone Bill	$1,200.00 per year (@$100.00 per month)	Complete Next Bill Due Jan 2026
Light/Gas/Water Bill	$2,400.00 per year (@ $200.00 per month)	Not Complete Next Bill Due May 2025

Tip #19

Manifest the Things You Want and Need by Speaking It Frequently

I know you may have heard people say things like this many times but may have dismissed it, DON'T, it works. Believe it or not, the majority of these steps are a form of manifestation, just in written form. Speaking the things you want out of life is so important, the bible says in Proverbs 18:21, *"The tongue can bring death or life; those who love to talk will reap the consequences."*

Have you ever noticed people who are always speaking negatively about everything tend to have lives that match that negativity? If you speak negatively over your relationship, children, finances, health, happiness, or job then don't expect to see it grow into something beautiful, and don't expect extraordinary things to come out of it. I have seen this negative mentality play out in more lives than I would like to, including mine at one point but, I have also lived and experienced life from the other side and I must say it is much more fulfilling. I have heard people say:

"I am never going to be able to pay off my debts."

"I am never going to be able to buy a house."

"We are never going to have enough money to save up."

"I will never be able to get my dream car."

"I will never get over my depression."

"I will never get married."

The more you say those things, the more you believe them, and the more your mind becomes blocked from producing them or coming up with solutions. When you choose to change your mindset and only speak positively you will see your entire world begin to change for the better.

For example, for years my husband would come home from work and check the mail and when he came in shuffling through it, I would say almost every day, "Did we get a $10,000 check yet?" and he would laugh and say, "nope not yet just some bills." Then one day years later I happened to check the mail this day and was on the phone with my husband and shuffled through the mail and said, "Bae? This looks like a check!" and when I opened it, to my surprise that is exactly what it was. Now it was not for $10,000 but it was for a little over $6,000 and what a blessing that was because it came right on time and confirmed to me once again that God's word is true. We are still manifesting that $10,000 check though, and now we know it is not impossible.

Another example is in 2011 I saw a Ford Flex and fell in love with it, and I would tell myself every time I passed one that one day, I will get that car. I would even drive past it and say, "Hey car I'll have you one day." For years I did that and in 2019 that is exactly what I got. Now that did not come without hard work and applying the tips provided to my daily life, but I hope it inspires you to speak the things you want out of life and believe for God to allow you to have them if it is in his will.

Tip #20

Put Your Money Back into Something

That Will Build Wealth

Last but certainly not least, invest your extra money into something that will build wealth. Once you get to this point where you have financial freedom, you want to make sure you make financial decisions that will keep you on that path but, on a bigger scale. For example, you can get into stocks, real estate, or start a business you always dreamed of (restaurant, salon, clothing store), anything that will allow your money to start working for you, instead of you working for it. As you continue to grow financially, continue to reinvest in yourself and your businesses.

BE BLESSED AND THANKS

Thank you for purchasing and taking the time to read my first book. I pray that these tips were exactly what you needed to get you started and I also pray it helps you tremendously on your financial journey.

"Your imagination is a preview of your lifetime coming attractions. If you can't imagine what it is going to be, don't ever expect to physically look in the mirror and see it."

Unknown

Other Books By Lekeyantia Naylor

20 Tips To Financial Success Personal Finance Journal

How I Wish

How I Wish Coloring Storybook

PUBLISHED BY

THELNBOOKS

TheLNBooks

www.thelnbooks.com

thelnbooks@gmail.com

www.ingramcontent.com/pod-product-compliance
Lightning Source LLC
Chambersburg PA
CBHW041715200326
41519CB00001B/173